Contents

Getting Help

Every effort has been made to ensure the accuracy of this book and the contents of its CD. If you do run into problems, please contact the appropriate source for help and assistance.

Getting Help with The Book and Its CD

Microsoft Press provides corrections for books and companion CDs through the World Wide Web at:

http://www.microsoft.com/learning/support/books/

To connect directly to the Microsoft Knowledge Base and enter a query regarding a question or issue that you may have, go to:

http://www.microsoft.com/learning/support/search.asp

Giving Feedback About the Book and Its CD

If you have comments, questions, or ideas regarding this book or its CD, or questions that are not answered by querying the Knowledge Base, please send them to Microsoft Press via e-mail to:

mspinput@microsoft.com

or via postal mail to:

Microsoft Press
Attn: Step by Step Editor
One Microsoft Way
Redmond, WA 98052-6399

Please note that product support is not offered through the above addresses.

Using the Book's CD

The CD included with this book contains all the practice files you'll use as you work through the book's exercises. By using the practice files, you won't waste time creating sample content with which to experiment–instead, you can jump right in and concentrate on learning how to create Web sites.

What's on the CD?

In addition to the practice files, the CD contains some resources that will really enhance your ability to get the most out of using this book, including the following:

- HTML color reference charts
- HTML and XHTML templates
- Bonus guides: "Designing for Accessibility" and "Designing for Usability"
- Microsoft Office System Quick Reference eBook
- Insider's Guide to Microsoft Office OneNote 2003 eBook
- Microsoft Computer Dictionary, Fifth Edition, eBook
- Introducing the Tablet PC eBook
- Complete HTML and XHTML Step by Step eBook

Minimum System Requirements

To complete the exercises in this book, you will need:

- **Computer/processor** Computer with a Pentium 133-megahertz (MHz) or higher processor; Pentium III recommended.
- **Memory** 64MB of RAM (128 MB recommended).
- **Drives** Hard drive and CD-ROM drive.
- **Hard disk** Hard disk requirements will vary depending on configuration; custom installation choices might require more or less hard disk space.
  - 245 MB of available hard disk space with 115 MB on the hard disk where the operating system is installed.
  - An additional 20 MB of hard disk space for installing the practice files.
- **Display** Super VGA (800 × 600) or higher-resolution monitor with 256 colors.

- **Pointing device** Microsoft Mouse, Microsoft IntelliMouse, or compatible pointing device.
- **Operating system** Microsoft Windows 2000 with Service Pack 3 (SP3) or Microsoft Windows XP Service Pack 2 or later.
- **Software** Microsoft Office FrontPage 2003, Microsoft Office Word 2003, and Microsoft Internet Explorer 6 or later.

Installing the Practice Files

You need to install the practice files on your hard disk before you use them in the chapters' exercises. Follow these steps.

1. Remove the companion CD from this book, and insert it into your CD-ROM drive.

   Note An end user license agreement should open automatically. If this agreement does not appear, open My Computer from the desktop or Start menu, double-click the icon for your CD-ROM drive, and then double-click StartCD.exe.

2. Review the end user license agreement. If you accept the terms, select the accept option, and then click **Next**.

   A menu will appear with options related to the book.

3. Click **Install Practice Files**.
4. Follow the instructions that appear.

   The code samples are installed to the following location on your computer:

   My Documents\Microsoft Press\HTML and XHTML SBS

Using the Practice Files

Each exercise is preceded by a paragraph or paragraphs that list the files needed for that exercise and explain any file preparation you need to take care of before you start working through the exercise.

The following table lists the practice file folders that you have installed from the CD. The practice file folder for each chapter includes a Solutions subfolder containing finished versions of the practice files used in that chapter.

Chapter	Folder	Subfolder
Chapter 1: HTML and XHTML Basics	01Basics	no subfolders
Chapter 2: Setting Up the Document Structure	02Structure	CreatingParagraphs SpecifyingKeywords PublishingFiles

Chapter	Folder	Subfolder
Chapter 3: Formatting Text by Using Tags	03Format	CreatingHeadings ApplyingBold ApplyingSuperscript UsingMonospace FormattingQuotes ConfiguringSettings
Chapter 4: Using Lists and Backgrounds	04Lists	NestingLists CreatingGlossary InsertingCharacters InsertingLines ChoosingColors SpecifyingImages
Chapter 5: Creating Hyperlinks and Anchors	05Links	CreatingHyperlinks LinkingEmail CreatingAnchors LinkingOther
Chapter 6: Introduction to Style Sheets	06Styles	ConstructingRules CreatingNested CreatingClasses StylingHyperlinks CreatingExternal
Chapter 7: Formatting Text by Using Style Sheets	07Text	SelectingFont SelectingSize ApplyingBold ApplyingStrike CreatingSpan AdjustingSpacing
Chapter 8: Formatting Paragraphs by Using Style Sheets	08Paragraphs	Indenting AddingBorders SettingAlignment AdjustingHeight
Chapter 9: Displaying Graphics	09Graphics	InsertingImages ClearingImages SizingImages CreatingHyperlinks UsingThumbnails UsingAlt

Chapter	Folder	Subfolder
Chapter 10: Creating Navigational Aids	10Navigation	CreatingTextBar CreatingGraphicBar CreatingImageMap Redirecting
Chapter 11: Creating Tables	11Tables	CreatingTable SpecifyingSize SettingWidth SpanningCells UsingTables
Chapter 12: Formatting Tables	12FmtTables	ApplyingBackground ApplyingBorders ChangingPadding CreatingGroups
Chapter 13: Creating Division-Based Layouts	13Divisions	CreatingDivisions PositioningDivisions FormattingDivisions
Chapter 14: Creating User Forms	14Forms	CreatingForms CreatingButtons CreatingLists
Chapter 15: Using Frames for Layout	15Frames	CreatingFramesets CreatingComplex SettingTargets FormattingFrames CreatingInline
Chapter 16: Incorporating Sound and Video	16Multimedia	RecordingSound LinkingSound EmbeddingSound EmbeddingVideo
Chapter 17: HTML and Microsoft Word	17Word	SavingFiles CreatingPages FormattingPages CreatingTables
Chapter 18: HTML and Microsoft FrontPage	18FrontPage	FromTemplate FromScratch ApplyingTheme CreatingNav

Uninstalling the Practice Files

After you finish working through this book, you should uninstall the practice files to free up hard disk space.

1. On the Windows taskbar, click the **Start** button, point to **Settings**, and then click **Control Panel**.
2. Double-click the **Add/Remove Programs** icon.
3. In the list of installed programs, click **HTML and XHTML Step by Step**, and then click **Add/Remove**.
4. Click **Yes** when the confirmation dialog box appears.

Conventions and Features

You can save time when you use this book by understanding how the *Step by Step* series shows special instructions, keys to press, buttons to click, and so on.

Convention	Meaning
(CD icon)	This icon indicates a reference to the book's companion CD.
BE SURE TO	These words are found at the beginning of paragraphs preceding or following step-by-step exercises. They point out items you should check or actions you should carry out either before beginning an exercise or after completing an exercise.
USE OPEN	These words are found at the beginning of paragraphs preceding step-by-step exercises. They draw your attention to practice files that you'll need to use in the exercise.
CLOSE	This word is found at the beginning of paragraphs following step-by-step exercises. They give instructions for closing open files or programs before moving on to another topic.
1 **2**	Numbered steps guide you through hands-on exercises in each topic.
●	A round bullet indicates an exercise that has only one step.
Troubleshooting	These paragraphs show you how to fix a common problem that might prevent you from continuing with the exercise.
Tip	These paragraphs provide a helpful hint or shortcut that makes working through a task easier.
Important	These paragraphs point out information that you need to know to complete a procedure.
Note	These paragraphs provide supplementary or related information.
Ctrl+C	A plus sign (+) between two key names means that youmust hold down the first key while you press the second key. For example, "press Ctrl+C" means "hold down the Ctrl key while you press the C key."
user interface elements	In exercises, the names of program elements such as buttons, commands, and dialog boxes.
user input	Anything you are supposed to type.
glossary terms	Terms explained in the glossary at the end of the book.

About the Author

Faithe Wempen, M.A., is a Computer Information Technology instructor at Indiana University/Purdue University at Indianapolis. She is a nationally known expert in PC hardware, A+ Certification preparation, and Microsoft Office.

Faithe has been writing about technology since 1995. Her authoring credits include over 90 books, translated into over a dozen languages, including *The PowerPoint 2003 Bible*, *Mastering Windows XP Professional*, and *Dell Guide to PC Fundamentals*. She has also authored several computer information technology textbooks, including *PC Maintenance: Preparing for A+ Certification* and *Learning Adobe InDesign CS2*, and written numerous articles for Web sites, including CertCities.com and TechProGuild.com, and featured cover stories for *Microsoft Office Solutions* and *Microsoft Office PRO* magazines.

Faithe is also a popular author and online instructor for Powered.com, for whom she develops and teaches courses on Microsoft Office applications, PC purchase and upgrade, home office setup and maintenance, and emerging hardware technologies. Her courses have educated more than a quarter of a million students through free online offerings for clients, including CNET, Hewlett-Packard, eMachines, Smead, and Sony.

Quick Reference

Abbreviations used in command syntax:

address An e-mail address

classname A class name you define

color A color expressed as a name, a hexadecimal value, or an RGB value

filename.ext A filename and extension

idname An ID name you define

n A digit

name A name assigned to a variable or anchor point

rule A style rule

tag Any tag (p, h1, h2, and so on)

text The text as it should appear onscreen

url A valid URL

value The value of a style rule

Chapter 1 HTML and XHTML Basics

Page 9

To open a Web page in Notepad

1. On the **Start** menu, point to **All Programs**, point to **Accessories**, and then click **Notepad**.
2. In the untitled Notepad window, on the **File** menu, click **Open**.
3. Navigate to the folder containing the file.
4. Click the **Files of type** arrow, and then click **All Files**.
5. In the **Open** dialog box, click the file, and then click **Open**.

Page 12

To preview a Web page in Microsoft Internet Explorer

1. On the **Start** menu, click **Internet Explorer**.
2. On the **File** menu, click **Open**.
3. Click the **Browse** button, and then browse to the folder containing the file.
4. Click the file, and then click **Open**.
5. Click **OK**.

Page 15

To save changes to a file in Notepad

- On the **File** menu, click **Save**.

Chapter 2 Setting Up the Document Structure

Page 20 **To specify a document type of transitional HTML 4.01**

```
<!DOCTYPE HTML PUBLIC "-//W3C/DTD HTML 4.01 Transitional//EN" "http://www.w3.org/
TR/html4/loose.dtd">
```

Page 20 **To specify a document type of transitional XHTML 1.0**

```
<!DOCTYPE HTML PUBLIC "-//W3C/DTD XHTML 1.0 Transitional//EN" "http://www.w3.org/
TR/xhtml1/DTD/xhtml1-transitional.dtd">
```

Page 21 **To create the HTML section**

```
<html></html>
```

Page 21 **To create the Head section (within the HTML section)**

```
<head></head>
```

Page 21 **To create the Body section (within the HTML section)**

```
<body></body>
```

Page 23 **To create a body paragraph**

```
<p>text</p>
```

Page 23 **To create a line break**

```
<br />
```

Page 26 **To create a page title (within the Head section)**

```
<title>text</title>
```

Page 26 **To create metatag keywords (within the Head section)**

```
<meta name="keywords" content="word1, word2, word3" />
```

Page 26 **To redirect the page to another URL**

```
<meta http=equiv="refresh" content="n; url="url" />
```

where *n* is a number of seconds of delay and *url* is the URL of the site to which to redirect.

Page 28 **To set up a Web location for publishing a Web site**

1. On the **Start** menu, click **My Network Places**.
2. In the **Network Tasks** area, click **Add a network place**, and then click **Next**.
3. Click **Choose another network location**, and then click **Next**.
4. Type the Web address to which you want to connect, including the http:// at the beginning, and then click **Next**.
5. If prompted, enter the user name and password you have been assigned for the server, and then click **OK**.
6. Type a name by which to refer to this network place, and then click **Next**.
7. Click **Finish**.

Page 28 **To save from Notepad directly to a Web location**

1. On the **File** menu, click **Save As**.
2. On the **Places** bar, click **My Network Places**, or click the **Save In** list, and then click **My Network Places**.
3. Double-click the network shortcut to the server.
4. If prompted, enter the user name and password required to connect to the server, and then click **OK**.
5. Browse to the folder in which you want to save the file.
6. If you want to see the files that are already there, click the **Save as type** arrow, and then click **All Files**.
7. Click **Save**.

Chapter 3 Formatting Text by Using Tags

Page 36 **To create headings (any of six levels)**

<h1> *text*</h1>
<h2> *text*</h2>
<h3> *text*</h3>
<h4> *text*</h4>
<h5> *text*</h5>
<h6> *text*</h6>

Optional argument:

`align=`	Sets horizontal alignment; valid values are `left`, `right`, `center`, and `justify`.

Page 38 **To apply bold to text**

<b> *text*</b>

Page 38 **To apply italics to text**

<i> *text*</i>

Page 40 **To apply superscript to text**

^{*text*}

Page 40 **To apply subscript to text**

_{*text*}

Page 41 **To apply monospace font to text**

<tt> *text*</tt>

or

<kbd> *text*</kbd>

or

<code> *text*</code>

or

```
<samp>text</samp>
```

Page 41 **To use preformatted text**

```
<pre>text</pre>
```

Page 48 **To create a block quotation**

```
<blockquote>text</blockquote>
```

Optional argument:

`cite=`	Specifies the URL source of the quote.

Page 52 **To change text viewing size in Internet Explorer**

- On the **View** menu, point to **Text Size**, and then click the size you want.

Page 52 **To change the default font for Web text in Internet Explorer**

1. On the **Tools** menu, click **Internet Options**.
2. On the **General** tab, click the **Fonts** button.
3. In the **Web page font** list, click the font you want.
4. In the **Plain text font** list, click the font you want.
5. Click **OK** in both the **Fonts** dialog box and the **Internet Options** dialog box.

Chapter 4 Using Lists and Backgrounds

Page 60 **To create an ordered (numbered) list**

```
<ol>
<li>text</li>
<li>text</li>
</ol>
```

Optional arguments:

`type=`	Specifies the number style; valid values are `decimal`, `decimal-leading-zero`, `lower-roman`, `upper-roman`, `lower-alpha`, `upper-alpha`, and `none`.
`start=`	Specifies the starting number; deprecated.

Page 60 **To create an item within an ordered or unordered list**

```
<li>text</li>
```

Optional argument:

`value=`	Specifies the number to be assigned to the list item (for ordered lists only); deprecated.

Page 60

To create an unordered (bulleted) list

```
<ul>
<li>text</li>
<li>text</li>
</ul>
```

Optional argument:

`type=`	Specifies the bullet style; valid values are `disc`, `circle`, and `square`.

Page 65

To create a definition list

```
<dl>
<dt>text</dt>
<dd>text text text</dt>
<dt>text</dt>
<dd>text text text</dt>
</dl>
```

Page 67

To insert common special characters

Symbol	Entity Name	Entity Number
& (ampersand)	&	&
< (less than)	<	<
> (greater than)	>	>
(nonbreaking space)		
¢ (cent)	¢	¢
£ (pound)	£	£
¥ (yen)	¥	¥
© (copyright)	©	©
® (registered trademark)	®	®
° (degree)	°	°
± (plus or minus)	±	±
† (dagger)	†	†
™ (trademark)	™	™

Page 68

To insert a horizontal line

```
<hr />
```

Optional style-based formatting:

```
<hr style="color: color; background-color: color; height: n; width: n" />
```

where *color* is a hexadecimal number, an RGB value, or a color name, and *n* is a number of pixels or a percentage.

Page 72 **To apply a page background color**

```
<body style="background-color: color">
```

where *color* is a color name, RGB value, or hexadecimal value.

Page 73 **To apply a foreground (text) color for the entire document**

```
<body style="color: color">
```

Page 73 **To use a background image file**

```
<body style="background-image: url(filename.ext)">
```

Chapter 5 Creating Hyperlinks and Anchors

Page 80 **To create a hyperlink**

```
<a href="URL">text</a>
```

Page 80 **To open the hyperlink in a new window**

```
<a href="URL" target="_blank">text</a>
```

Page 83 **To add a hyperlink to an e-mail address**

```
<a href="mailto:address" target="_blank">text</a>
```

Optional argument:

`subject=`	Specifies a default subject line.

Page 87 **To create an anchor point**

```
<a name="name">text</a>
```

Page 87 **To reference an anchor point in a hyperlink**

```
<a href="#name">text</a>
```

Chapter 6 Introduction to Style Sheets

Page 97 **To apply a style to an individual tag (for example, <h1>)**

```
<tag style="rule: value; rule: value">text</tag>
```

where *tag* is any tag, *rule* is a style rule, and *value* is the value for that rule.

Page 97 **To create an internal style sheet for the document**

```
<head>
<style>
tag {rule: value; rule: value}
</style>
</head>
```

where *tag* is any tag, *rule* is a style rule, and *value* is the value for that rule. For example:

```
p {font-size: 10px; font-color: blue}
```

Page 100

To create a style rule for a nested tag

For example, if *tag2* should be formatted a certain way only when nested inside *tag1*:

```
<head>
<style>
tag1 tag2 {rule: value; rule: value}
</style>
</head>
```

where *tag1* and *tag2* are any tags, *rule* is a style rule, and *value* is the value for that rule. Example: for bold text within a paragraph:

```
p b {font-weight: bold; font-color: blue}
```

Page 103

To create a formatting class

```
<head>
<style>
.classname {rule: value; rule: value}
</style>
</head>
```

where *classname* is a name you assign, *rule* is a style rule, and *value* is the value for that rule. For example:

```
.new {font-color: red; font-weight: bold}
```

Page 103

To apply a formatting class to a tag

```
<tag class="classname">text</tag>
```

where *classname* is a name you assign and *tag* is any tag. For example:

```
<p class="new">Now available!</p>
```

Page 103

To create a formatting ID

```
<head>
<style>
#idname {rule: value; rule: value}
</style>
</head>
```

where *idname* is a name you assign, *rule* is a style rule, and *value* is the value for that rule. For example:

```
#firstitem {font-size: 10px; font-weight: bold}
```

Page 103

To apply a formatting ID to a tag

```
<tag id="idname">text</tag>
```

where *idname* is a name you assign and *tag* is any tag. For example:

```
<p id="firstitem">Now available!</p>
```

Page 105 **To create style rules for hyperlink formatting**

```
<head>
<style>
a:link {rule: value}
a:visited {rule: value}
a:hover {rule: value}
a:active {rule: value}
</style>
</head>
```

where *rule* is a style rule and *value* is the value for that rule. For example:

```
a:link {font-color: pink}
```

Page 108 **To create an external style sheet**

1. Start a new document in Notepad.
2. Type style rules in this format:

   ```
   tag {rule: value; rule: value}
   ```

3. Save the file by using a .css extension.
4. In an HTML document, add this line to the Head section:

   ```
   <link rel="stylesheet" type="text/css" href="filename.css">
   ```

   where *filename.css* is the name of the file you created in step 3.

Chapter 7 Formatting Text by Using Style Sheets

Page 114 **To assign a font**

Within the tag:

```
<tag style="font-family: font1, font2, font3">text</tag>
```

where *tag* is any tag and *font1*, *font2*, and *font3* are different fonts. (*font2* and *font3* are optional.) For example:

```
<p style="font-family: helvetica, arial">Now available!</p>
```

In a style sheet:

```
tag {font-family: "font1", "font2", "font3"}
```

where *tag* is any tag and *font1*, *font2*, and *font3* are different fonts. (*font2* and *font3* are optional.) For example:

```
p {font-family: helvetica, arial}
```

Page 117 **To assign a font size**

Within the tag:

```
<tag style="font-size: npx">text</tag>
```

where *n* is a number of pixels, such as `10`. Other acceptable units of measure are `in` (inches), `cm` (centimeters), `mm` (millimeters), `pt` (points), and `pc` (picas). For example:

```
<p style="font=size: 12pt">Now available!</p>
```

Alternate methods of expressing size:

- **Relational descriptions.** Where *size* is a relational description: `xx-small`, `x-small`, `small`, `medium`, `large`, `x-large`, or `xx-large`.
- **Multipliers.** Such as *n*em, where *n* is a multiplier of the base font. For example, 2em is 200%.
- **Percentages.** Such as *n*% where *n* is a percentage of the base font. For example, 200%.

Style sheet:

```
tag {font-size: npx}
```

where *n* is a number of pixels, such as `10`. Other acceptable units of measure are `in` (inches), `cm` (centimeters), `mm` (millimeters), `pt` (points), and `pc` (picas).

You can also use any of the alternative methods for expressing size shown under "Within the tag."

Page 117

To assign a font color

Within the tag:

```
<tag style="color: color">text</tag>
```

where *color* is a color name, an RGB value, or a hexadecimal value. Examples:

```
<p style="color: blue">text</p>
<p style="color: 0,0,255">text</p>
<p style="color: 0000FF">text</p>
```

In a style sheet:

```
tag {color: color}
```

where *color* is a color name, an RGB value, or a hexadecimal value. Examples:

```
p {color: blue}
p {color: 0,0,255}
p {color: 0000FF}
```

Page 120

To apply bold to text by using a style

Within the tag:

```
<tag style="font-weight: bold">text</tag>
```

where *tag* is any tag. For example:

```
<p style="font-weight: bold">Now available!</p>
```

In a style sheet:

```
tag {font-weight: bold}
```

Page 120

To apply italics to text by using a style

Within the tag:

```
<tag style="font-style: italic">text</tag>
```

In a style sheet:

```
tag {font-style: italic}
```

Page 123 **To apply strikethrough to text**

Within the tag:

```
<tag style="text-decoration: line-through">text</tag>
```

In a style sheet:

```
tag {text-decoration: line-through}
```

Page 123 **To apply underlining to text**

Within the tag:

```
<tag style="text-decoration: underline">text</tag>
```

In a style sheet:

```
tag {text-decoration: underline}
```

Page 123 **To remove inherited text decoration**

Within the tag:

```
<tag style="text-decoration: none">text</tag>
```

In a style sheet:

```
tag {text-decoration: none}
```

Page 126 **To create an inline span**

1. Surround the text to be spanned with a two-sided <span> tag. For example:

   ```
   This is <span>great fun</span>.
   ```

2. Apply style rules to the opening span tag. Example:

   ```
   This is <span style="font-weight: bold">great fun</span>
   ```

Page 127 **To adjust spacing between letters**

Within the tag:

```
<tag style="letter-spacing: npx">text</tag>
```

where *tag* is any tag and *n* is a number of pixels. For example:

```
<p style="letter-spacing: 1px">Now available!</p>
```

In a style sheet:

```
tag {letter-spacing: npx}
```

Page 127 **To adjust spacing between words**

Within the tag:

```
<tag style="word-spacing: npx">text</tag>
```

where *tag* is any tag and *n* is a number of pixels. For example:

```
<p style="word-spacing: 2px">Now available!</p>
```

In a style sheet:

```
tag {word-spacing: npx}
```

Chapter 8 Formatting Paragraphs by Using Style Sheets

Page 133

To apply a first-line indent

Within the tag:

```
<tag style="text-indent: npx">text</tag>
```

where *tag* is any tag and *n* is a number of pixels. For example:

```
<p style="text-indent: 20px">Now available!</p>
```

In a style sheet:

```
tag {text-indent: npx}
```

Page 133

To apply padding (space inside an element)

Expand paragraph border (Effects borders)

Within the tag:

```
<tag style="padding: npx">text</tag>
```

where *tag* is any tag and *n* is a number of pixels. For example:

```
<p style="padding: 5px">Now available!</p>
```

In a style sheet:

```
tag {padding: npx}
```

Page 133

To apply a margin (space outside an element)

Expand margin outside paragraph border

Within the tag:

```
<tag style="margin: npx">text</tag>
```

where *tag* is any tag and *n* is a number of pixels. For example:

```
<p style="margin: 5px">Now available!</p>
```

In a style sheet:

```
tag {margin: npx}
```

Page 137

To apply a paragraph border

Within the tag:

```
<tag style="border-style: style">text</tag>
```

where *tag* is any tag and *style* is one of these: `solid`, `dotted`, `dashed`, `double`, `groove`, `ridge`, `inset`, `outset`, or none.

In a style sheet:

```
tag {border-style: style}
```

Optional additional border-related rules:

`padding`	Changes the amount of space between the inner content and the border.
`border-width`	Changes the thickness of the border.
`border-color`	Changes the color of the border.

Page 137

To specify border attributes for all sides at once

Use the border attribute, and then specify the settings in this order: *size*, *color*, *style*. For example:

```
<p style="border: 2px green solid">
```

Page 137

To format individual sides of a paragraph border

Include `-top`, `-right`, `-left`, or `-bottom` between the word *border* and the property being set. Examples:

```
<p style="border-top-style: dashed">
<p style="border-bottom-color: blue">
```

Page 142

To align a paragraph horizontally

Within the tag:

```
<tag style="text-align: style">text</tag>
```

where *tag* is any tag and *style* is one of these: `left`, `center`, `right`, or `justify`.

In a style sheet:

```
tag {text-align: style}
```

Page 144

To specify vertical spacing within a paragraph (leading)

Within the tag:

```
<tag style="line-height: n">text</tag>
```

where *tag* is any tag and *n* is a number in pixels, such as `3px`, or a percentage, such as `200%`.

In a style sheet:

```
tag {line-height: n}
```

Chapter 9 Displaying Graphics

Page 150

To insert an image

```
<img src="filename.ext" />
```

To refer to a file that is up one level in the folder structure:

```
<img src="../filename.ext" />
```

Page 150

To wrap text around an image and force the image to the left or right side of the screen

Within the tag:

```
<img src="filename.ext" style="float: left" />
```

or

```
<img src="filename.ext" style="float: right" />
```

In a style sheet:

```
img {float: left}
```

or

```
img {float: right}
```

Page 152 **To delay text vertically until it is clear of an earlier graphic**

```
<tag style="clear: left">text</tag>
```

or

```
<tag style="clear: right">text</tag>
```

where *tag* is any text-related tag such as <p> or <h1>.

Page 154 **To specify an image size**

To specify height only (width changes proportionally):

```
<img src="filename.ext" height="n" />
```

where *n* is a number of pixels.

To specify width only (height changes proportionally):

```
<img src="filename.ext" width="n" />
```

where *n* is a number of pixels.

To specify both height and width (picture can distort):

```
<img src="filename.ext" height="n" width="n" />
```

where *n* is a number of pixels.

Page 157 **To use a graphic as a hyperlink**

```
<a href="url"><img src="filename.ext"></a>
```

Page 162 **To include alternative text for an image**

```
<img src="filename.ext" alt="text" />
```

where *text* is the text that should display in a pop-up when the visitor points at the image.

Chapter 10 Creating Navigational Aids

Page 170 **To create a text-based navigation bar**

1. Type the text for the hyperlinks. If needed, insert additional spaces between them by using ` ` codes.
2. Change each of the words or phrases into a hyperlink. (See "To create a hyperlink" in the Chapter 5 section of this Quick Reference.)

Page 173 **To create a graphical navigation bar**

1. Insert the images to be used for the navigation bar. (See "To insert an image" in the Chapter 9 section of this Quick Reference.) If needed, insert additional spaces between them by using ` ` codes.
2. Change each image into a hyperlink. (See "To use a graphic as a hyperlink" in the Chapter 9 section of this Quick Reference.)

3 (Optional) Add alternative text for each hyperlink. (See "To include alternative text for an image" in the Chapter 9 section of this Quick Reference.

Page 175 **To create an image map (rectangular)**

1 Insert the image to be used for the map's graphic. (See "To insert an image" in the Chapter 9 section of this Quick Reference.)

2 Immediately after the image's tag, create an image map:

```
<map name="name" id="name">
</map>
```

where *name* is a name you assign to uniquely identify this map within the document.

3 Within the <map> tag, create hot spots:

```
<area shape="rect" coords="x1,y1,x2,y2" href="url" />
```

where *x1* and *y1* are the number of pixels horizontally and vertically from the upper-left corner of the image for the upper-left corner of the hot spot, and *x2* and *y2* are the number of pixels from the upper-left corner of the image for the lower-right corner of the hot spot.

4 Repeat step 3 to create all the hot spots needed.

Page 175 **To create an image map (circular)**

1 Insert the image to be used for the map's graphic. (See "To insert an image" in the Chapter 9 section of this Quick Reference.

2 Immediately after the image's tag, create an image map:

```
<map name="name" id="name">
</map>
```

where *name* is a name you assign to uniquely identify this map within the document.

3 Within the <map> tag, create hot spots:

```
<area shape="circle" coords="x1, y1, r" href="url" />
```

where *x1* and *y1* are the number of pixels horizontally and vertically from the upper-left corner of the image for the center point of the circle, and *r* is the radius of the circle in pixels.

Page 175 **To create an image map (polygonal)**

1 Insert the image to be used for the map's graphic. (See "To insert an image" in the Chapter 9 section of this Quick Reference.)

2 Immediately after the image's tag, create an image map:

```
<map name="name" id="name">
</map>
```

where *name* is a name you assign to uniquely identify this map within the document.

3 Within the <map> tag, create hot spots:

```
<area shape="circle" coords="x1, y1, x2, y2, x3, y3..." href="url" />
```

where each pair of *x* and *y* coordinates are points from the upper-left corner of the image.

Page 181 **To redirect a page to another URL**

Place this code within the Head section of the document:

```
<meta http-equiv="refresh" content="n" url="url" />
```

where *n* is a number of seconds of delay and *url* is the URL of the site to which you want to redirect.

Chapter 11 Creating Tables

Page 186 **To create a table**

1 Create a table tag:

```
<table>
</table>
```

2 Insert row tags for as many rows as you need:

```
<table>
    <tr></tr>
    <tr></tr>
</table>
```

3 Within each row, insert table cell tags for as many cells as you need:

```
<tr>
    <td></td>
    <td></td>
</tr>
```

4 Type text and/or insert other content, such as images, between the opening and closing table cell tags:

```
<td>text</td>
<td><img src="filename.ext" /></td>
```

Page 190 **To specify the width of a table**

Within the tag:

```
<table width=n>
```

where *n* is a percentage (such as `100%`) or a number of pixels (such as `600px`).

In a style sheet:

```
table {width=n}
```

Page 190 **To specify the height of a table**

Within the tag:

```
<table height=n>
```

where *n* is a percentage (such as `100%`) or a number of pixels (such as `600px`).

In a style sheet:

```
table {height=n}
```

Page 196 **To specify the width of a column within a table**

Add a `width=` argument to the cell's opening tag in the first row (or any row):

```
<td width=n>
```

where *n* is a percentage (such as `100%`) or a number of pixels (such as `600px`).

Page 200 **To merge cells**

```
<td 200="n">
```

where *n* is a number of columns to span, or

```
<td rowspan="n">
```

where *n* is a number of rows to span.

Chapter 12 Formatting Tables

Page 209 **To apply a border to a table**

Argument method:

```
<table border="n">
```

where *n* is a number of pixels.

Style method:

```
<table style="border-style: type; border-width=n">
```

where *type* is one of the following values: `solid`, `dotted`, `dashed`, `double`, `groove`, `ridge`, `inset`, `outset`, or `none`.

Page 209 **To assign a color to a table border**

Argument method:

```
<table border="n" bordercolor="color">
```

where *color* is a color expressed as a name, an RGB value, or a hexadecimal number.

Style method:

```
<table style="border-style: style; border-color: color">
```

where *color* is a color expressed as a name, an RGB value, or a hexadecimal number.

Page 209

To apply the width, color, and style of a border by using a single command

```
<table style="border: n,color,style">
```

where *n* is a number of pixels in width, *color* is a color expressed as a name, an RGB value, or a hexadecimal number, and *style* is one of these values: `solid`, `dotted`, `dashed`, `double`, `groove`, `ridge`, `inset`, `outset`, or `none`.

Page 209

To apply a border to only certain outer edges of a table

```
<table border="n" frame="value">
```

where *value* is one of the following values: `above`, `below`, `border`, `box`, `hsides`, `vsides`, `lhs`, `rhs`, or `void`.

Page 209

To apply a border to specific inner edges of a table

```
<table border="n" rules="value">
```

where *value* is one of the following values: `all`, `cols`, `rows`, `none`, or `groups`.

Page 218

To apply background color to a table, row, or cell

```
<tag style="background-color: color">
```

where *tag* is `table`, `tr`, or `td` and *color* is a color expressed as a name, an RGB value, or a hexadecimal number.

Page 218

To apply foreground (text) color to a table, row, or cell

```
<tag style=" color: color">
```

where *tag* is `table`, `tr`, or `td` and *color* is a color expressed as a name, an RGB value, or a hexadecimal number.

Page 218

To apply a background image to a table, row, or cell

```
<tag style=" background-image: url(filename.ext)">
```

where *tag* is `table`, `tr`, or `td`.

Page 222

To set cell padding for the entire table

```
<table cellpadding="npx">
```

where *n* is a number of pixels, such as `4px`.

Page 222

To set cell padding for an individual cell

Within the tag:

```
<td style="padding: npx">
```

where *n* is a number of pixels, such as `4px`.

In a style sheet:

```
td {padding: n}
```

where *n* is a number of pixels, such as `4px`.

Page 222 **To set cell spacing for the entire table**

```
<table cellspacing="npx">
```

where *n* is a number of pixels, such as 4px.

Page 222 **To set horizontal alignment for a cell**

Argument method:

```
<td align="value">
```

where *value* is left, right, center, or justify.

Style method, within the tag:

```
<td style="text-align: value">
```

where *value* is left, right, center, or justify.

In a style sheet:

```
td {text-align: value}
```

where *value* is left, right, center, or justify.

Page 222 **To set vertical alignment for a cell**

Argument method:

```
<td valign="value">
```

where *value* is top, bottom, or middle.

Style method, within the tag:

```
<td style="vertical-align: value">
```

where *value* is top, bottom, or middle.

In a style sheet

```
td {vertical-align: value}
```

where *value* is top, bottom, or middle.

Page 225 **To create a column group**

As a one-sided tag:

```
<colgroup span="n" style="rule: value" />
```

where *n* is the number of columns to span, *rule* is a style rule, and *value* is the value for that rule.

As a two-sided tag:

```
<colgroup span="n" style="rule: value">
<col style="rule: value" />
<col style="rule: value" />
</colgroup>
```

where *n* is the number of columns to span, *rule* is a style rule, and *value* is the value for that rule.

Chapter 13 Creating Division-Based Layouts

Page 231 **To create a division**

```
<div id="name">
</div>
```

where *name* is a unique ID within the document for each division.

Page 235 **To float a division to the left or right**

```
<div id="name" style="float: left">
```

or

```
<div id="name" style="float: right">
```

Page 235 **To position a division absolutely with respect to the parent element**

```
<div id="name" style="position: absolute; top: n; left: n">
```

where *n* is the number of pixels of offset vertically and horizontally from the upper-left corner of the parent element.

Page 235 **To position a division offset from its natural position**

```
<div id="name" style="position: relative; top: n; left: n">
```

where *n* is the number of pixels of offset vertically and horizontally from the position at which it would otherwise appear.

Page 235 **To position a division at a fixed location**

```
<div id="name" style="position: fixed; top: n; left: n">
```

where *n* is the number of pixels of offset vertically and horizontally from the upper-left corner of the page when displayed in a browser. Internet Explorer does not support this setting.

Chapter 14 Creating User Forms

Page 248 **To create a user input form**

```
<form method="post">
</form>
```

Page 248 **To send form results to an e-mail address**

```
<form method="post" action=mailto:emailaddress enctype="text/plain">
```

where *emailaddress* is the address to which to send the data.

Page 248 **To send form results to a CGI script**

```
<form method="post" action="url">
```

where *url* is the path to the script.

Page 248 **To create a text box field in a form**

```
<input type="text" name="fieldname" size="n" maxlength="n" />
```

where *fieldname* is a unique name you assign, and *n* is a number of characters.

Page 248 **To create a multiline text area**

```
<textarea name="fieldname" rows="n1" columns="n2">Default text</textarea>
```

where *fieldname* is a unique name you assign, *n1* is a number of rows of height, and *n2* is a number of characters of width.

Page 248 **To create a Submit button**

```
<input type="submit" value="text" />
```

where *text* is the text that should appear on the button face (such as Submit or Send).

Page 248 **To create a Reset button**

```
<input type="reset" value="text" />
```

where *text* is the text that should appear on the button face (such as Reset or Clear).

Page 252 **To create a check box**

```
<input type="checkbox" name="text" />
```

where *text* is a unique name you assign.

Optional arguments:

`value=`	Specifies the text to be returned if the check box is marked.
`checked="checked"`	Sets the default on/off state to On.

Page 252 **To create a set of option buttons**

```
<input type="radio" name="name" value="value">
```

where *name* is the common (shared) name for all option buttons in the group and *value* is the unique name for that button. Example:

```
<input type="radio" name="medal" value="gold" />Gold
<input type="radio" name="medal" value="silver" />Silver
```

Page 255 **To create a menu**

```
<select name="name" size="n">
<option>Text1</option>
<option>Text2</option>
</select>
```

where *name* is the name you assign for the menu, *n* is the height of the menu box in rows, and *Text1* and *Text2* are the items to appear on the menu.

Chapter 15 Using Frames for Layout

Page 264 **Specify the document type for a frameset**

```
<!DOCTYPE HTML PUBLIC "-//W3C//DTD HTML 4.01 Frameset//EN" "http://www.w3.org/TR/
html4/frameset.dtd">
```

Page 267

Create a frameset

```
<html>
<frameset>
<frame src="filename1.ext" name="name1">
<frame src=" filename2.ext" name="name2">
</frameset>
</html>
```

Page 267

Specify the widths of the frameset columns

```
<frameset cols="n1, n2">
```

where *n1* and *n2* are numbers of pixels or * (asterisk) representing a resizable column. You can have as many or as few columns as you want.

Page 267

Specify the heights of the frameset rows

```
<frameset rows="n1, n2">
```

where *n1* and *n2* are numbers of pixels or * (asterisk) representing a resizable row. You can have as many or as few rows as you want.

Page 267

Provide a no-frames alternative in the frameset document

```
<noframes>
<body>
Text message to appear when frames cannot be displayed
</body>
</noframes>
```

Page 274

Set the default target frame for all hyperlinks on a page

Place in Head section:

```
<base target="name">
```

where *name* is the name of the default target frame as specified in the frame's `name=` argument.

Page 274

Set the target to frame a hyperlink

```
<a href="url" target="name">Text</a>
```

where *name* is the frame name specified in the `name=` argument for the frame's opening tag or one of these values:

`target="_blank"`	Opens the hyperlink in a new window.
`target="_self"`	Opens the hyperlink in the same window.
`target="_top"`	Abandons the frameset and displays the page in a full browser window.
`target="_parent"`	Abandons one level of frameset. Same as `target="_top"` except when using nested framesets.

Page 281 **Set an inline frame**

```
<iframe src="url">Content to appear if the browser does not support inline
frames</iframe>
```

Chapter 16 Incorporating Audio and Video

Page 293 **To optimize the microphone recording level in Microsoft Windows**

1. On the **Start** menu, click Control Panel.
2. Do one of the following:
   - If Control Panel is in **Category** view (blue background), click **Sounds, Speech, and Audio Devices**, and then click **Speech**.
   - If Control Panel is in **Classic** view (white background), double-click **Speech**.
3. In the **Speech Properties** dialog box, click **Configure Microphone** to start the **Microphone Wizard**.
4. On the **Welcome** page, click **Next** to continue.
5. Read the sentence shown on the **Adjust Volume** page in a normal tone of voice until the message "Your microphone volume level is now tuned to your voice" appears in the dialog box, and then click **Next**.
6. Read the sentence shown on the **Test Positioning** page, and then wait for it to be played back to you. If necessary, adjust the microphone's position in relation to your mouth and try again until you are comfortable with the playback, and then click **Finish**.
7. Click **OK** to close the **Speech Properties** dialog box, and then close Control Panel.

Page 293 **To record narration by using Sound Recorder**

1. Click **Start**, point to **All Programs**, **Accessories**, and **Entertainment**, and then click **Sound Recorder**.
2. In the Sound Recorder window, click the **Record** button (labeled with a red circle), and then speak into the microphone.
3. When you are finished, click the **Stop** button (labeled with a black square).
4. Click the **Play** button (labeled with a right-pointing triangle), and then listen to the recording.
5. Re-record if needed. When you are satisfied with your recording, on the **File** menu, click **Save**.
6. In the **Save As** dialog box, navigate to the folder in which you want to save the file.
7. In the **File name** box, type welcome.
8. Click **Save**.

Page 296 **To create a hyperlink to an audio or video clip**

```
<a href="filename.ext">text</a>
```

where *filename.ext* is the audio or video clip and *text* is the text to appear as the hyperlink.

Page 298 **To embed an audio or video clip**

`<embed src="filename.ext" />`

where *filename.ext* is the audio or video clip.

Optional arguments:

`autostart=`	Specifies whether the clip starts automatically. Valid values are `false` and `true`.
`width=`	Specifies the width of a video playback window, in pixels.
`height=`	Specifies the height of a video playback window, in pixels.
`loop=`	Specifies the number of repeats. Valid values are `infinite`, `true`, `false`, and all integers.
`alt=`	Specifies alternative text that should appear if the video clip cannot be displayed.

Page 298 **To embed a background sound (no controls)**

`<bgsound src="filename.ext">`

Optional arguments:

`loop=`	Specifies the number of repeats. Valid values are `infinite`, `true`, `false`, and all integers.
`volume=`	Specifies a clip volume, from 0 (muted) to 10,000 (loudest).

Chapter 17 HTML and Microsoft Word

Page 309 **To save a Word document as a Web page**

1. In Word, on the **File** menu, click **Save as Web Page**.
2. In the **Save as type** list, click the type you want:
   - **Web Page**
   - **Web Page, Filtered**
   - **Single File Web Page**
3. In the **File name** box, type the name you want, and then click the **Change Title** button.
4. Type a title for the page, click **OK**, and then click **Save**. If a warning box appears, click **Continue**.

Page 316 **To start a new Web page in Word**

1. On the **File** menu, click **New**.
2. In the **New Document** task pane, click **Web page**.

Page 316 **To apply a style in Word**

1. Click in the line of text to which you want to apply the style.
2. From the **Style** list on the Formatting toolbar, select a style.

Page 316 **To make more styles available in Word**

1. On the **Formatting** toolbar, click the **Styles and Formatting** button.
2. In the **Show** list at the bottom of the **Styles and Formatting** task pane, click **All styles**.

Page 316 **To insert a picture in Word**

1. On the **Insert** menu, point to **Picture**, and then click **From File**.
2. In the **Insert Picture** dialog box, navigate to the folder containing the picture, select the picture file, and then click **Insert**.

Page 316 **To insert an e-mail hyperlink in Word**

1. Select the text to be used for the hyperlink.
2. Press Ctrl+K to begin creating a new hyperlink.
3. Click the **E-mail Address** button.
4. In the **E-mail address** box, type the e-mail address, and then click **OK**.

Page 316 **To insert a Web hyperlink in Word**

1. Select the text to be used for the hyperlink.
2. Press Ctrl+K to begin creating a new hyperlink.
3. In the **Address** box, type the URL, and then click **OK**.

Page 321 **To insert a horizontal line in Word**

1. On the **Format** menu, click **Borders and Shading**.
2. Click the **Horizontal Line** button.
3. Click the line you want, and then click **OK**.

Page 321 **To apply a formatting theme in Word**

1. On the **Format** menu, click **Theme**.
2. Click a theme, and then click **OK** to apply it.

Page 325 **To create a table in Word**

- Click the **Insert Table** button, and then drag across the grid to select the number of rows and columns you want.

Chapter 18 HTML and Microsoft FrontPage

Page 334 **To view the site's navigational structure**

1. In the status bar at the bottom of the FrontPage window, click **Navigation**, or open the **View** menu and click **Navigation**.
2. If you want to change the structure, drag-and-drop pages to the locations you want.
3. If you want to delete a page, select a page, and then press **Delete**.

Page 334 **To change the view of a page**

- Click one of these buttons in the status bar at the bottom of the window:
  - Preview
  - Code
  - Split

Page 336 **To create a FrontPage Web site from a template**

1. In FrontPage, if the **New** task pane does not appear, on the **File** menu, click **New**.
2. In the **New Web Site** area, click **More Web site templates**.
3. In the **Web Site Templates** dialog box, click **Personal Web Site**.
4. Click the **Browse** button to open the **New Web Site Location** dialog box.
5. Navigate to the location where you want to save your site, and then click **Open**.
6. In the **Web Site Templates** dialog box, click **OK**.

Page 336 **Rename a page in the navigation structure**

1. Right-click a box, and then click **Rename**.
2. Type the new name, and then press Enter.

Page 336 **To remove a hyperlink**

1. Right-click the hyperlink, and then click **Hyperlink Properties**.
2. In the **Edit Hyperlink** dialog box, click **Remove Link**.

Page 339 **To start an empty Web site in FrontPage**

1. If the New task pane does not appear, on the **File** menu, click **New**.
2. Click **More Web site templates**.
3. Click **Empty Web site**.
4. Click the **Browse** button to open the New Web Site Location dialog box.
5. Navigate to the folder where you want to store the site, and then click **Open**.
6. In the **Web Site Templates** dialog box, click **OK**.

Page 339

To create a new Web page within a site

1. On the **File** menu, click **New**.
2. In the **New** task pane, click **Blank Page**.
3. On the **File** menu, click **Save As**.
4. In the **Save As** dialog box, click the **Change Title** button.
5. In the **Page title** box of the **Set Page Title** dialog box, type a title for the page, and then click **OK**.
6. In the **Save As** dialog box, click **Save**.

Page 343

To apply a formatting theme in FrontPage

1. On the **Format** menu, click **Theme**.
2. In the **Theme** task pane, scroll through the themes and double-click the theme you want.

Page 345

To create a navigation bar based on the site structure

1. Click where you want the navigation bar to appear.
2. From the **Insert** menu, click **Navigation**.
3. In the **Choose a bar type** list of the **Insert Web Component** dialog box, click **Bar based on navigation structure**, and then click **Next**.
4. In the **Choose a bar style** area, leave **Use Page's Theme** selected or select a different theme. Click **Next**.
5. In the **Choose an orientation** list, click the orientation you want.
6. Click **Finish**.
7. In the **Hyperlinks to add to page** section of the **Link Bar Properties** dialog box, leave **Child level** selected.
8. If you want to include the home page on the navigation bar, select the **Home page** check box, and then click **OK**.

I
Getting Started with HTML

Open a Web page in Notepad,
page 9

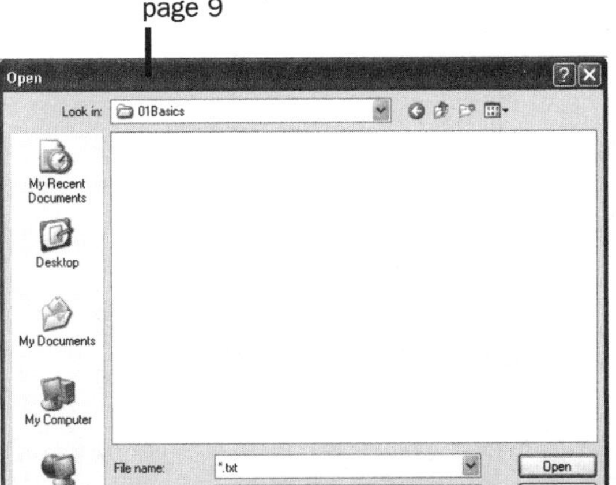

Preview a Web page in Internet Explorer,
page 12

Make, save, and view changes,
page 15

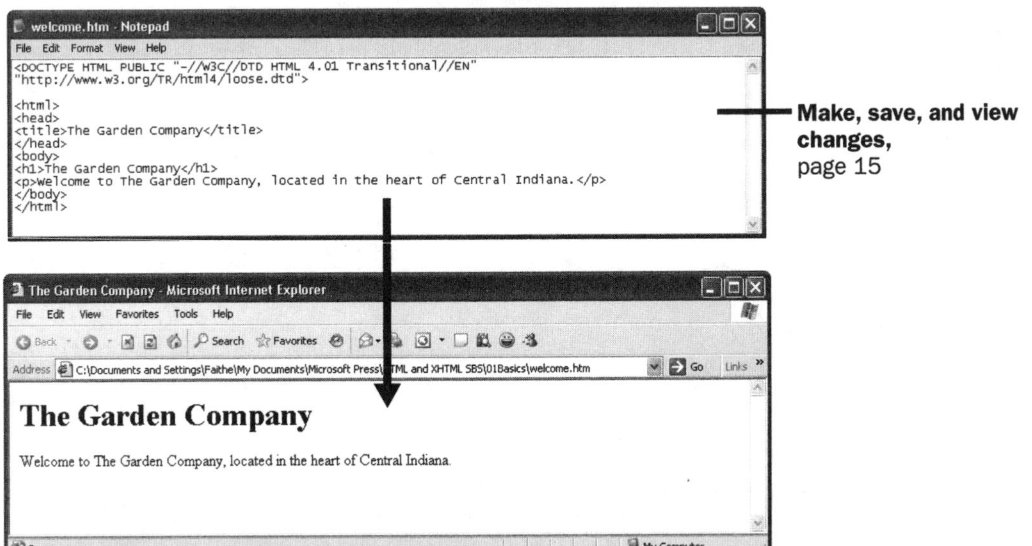

Chapter 1 at a Glance